MW01377321

GAMA

GAMA

Paul Powell

ATHENA PRESS
LONDON

GAMA
Copyright © Paul Powell

ISBN 1 84401 692 7

First Published 2006 by
ATHENA PRESS
Queen's House, 2 Holly Road
Twickenham TW1 4EG
United Kingdom

Printed for Athena Press

Introduction

Having waited for some time for a sign to encourage me to start writing this book, I one day realised that the sign had come and gone without me noticing because of my own over-enthusiasm.

For some time I had thought about putting pen to paper, but had not had the courage and did not know where to start or how to say what it was that was needing to be said or that I was the person to say it. I would have been rather stupid not to make a start, for if I had not, then the thoughts that were going through my head would have ended up never being heard and therefore wasted. There is so much to say and I only hope that I will be able to convey the message in a full and comprehensive manner.

During the course of this book and in each chapter I hope to be able to relay to you my hopes and dreams, not just idle dreams or hopeless thoughts, but the careful consideration of ideas. I have the intention of conveying my beliefs and inspirations, these will be conveyed in honesty and truth, not the fantasies of a romantic idealist, but reality, life, the perception of one who seeks to take the opportunity given to share with others that which would otherwise have passed by in solemnity and withered and died.

I would like to thank all those who have helped in writing this book, those from this world and those from the world beyond, for all the care and inspiration that I so dearly need, for giving me the courage to be able to share my life with others.

Each and everyone who reads this book must make up their own mind whether or not it is the truth.

Life eternal begins but with one step, after that eternal progress is the responsibility of the individual.

CHAPTER ONE

Today I talk with you of the Spirit within, a special gift to be nurtured and cared for. If we do not, we will not progress beyond that which we see in our daily material world with the physical seeing eye. Tell me my friends how often do we sit and think about the direction in which we think our lives should be, or are intended to go... too often, I fear, for if we were to trust in the divine and natural Law given to us by our Creator, we would have no need to sit and ponder, searching aimlessly in the mist of our clouded thoughts, stumbling in the shadows of our crowded minds. There is a clear pathway for us all to tread, a pathway that is clearer than crystal, it is so obvious that we cannot see it, because we are looking straight through it, it is all around us all the time, waiting and waiting for us to reach out and touch it.

Life itself is our meaning for being here, not the meaning of life. Let me explain. Every day when we wake in the morning we do not question why the sun rises in the sky because we know that it has done, and will do so for time immemorial, we do not sit and pray for the sun to rise in the normal sense every morning, we trust, because we know that it will.

Why then do we have to plan and ask questions in order that we feel we are making progress, when progress is as natural and normal as a sunrise; too many questions answered wrongly, too many answers questioned wrongly. If we as right thinking minds did as natural Law required, we would be given the knowledge to be able to realise our own individual paths, thus enabling us to help those who seek the path and thereby expand the conscious, universal mind, making mankind better able to understand one another, have respect for all life and the Laws which govern it, filling the world with the responsibility to give consideration to all living things, so that eternal progress is open to all and not just the human race or the privileged that reside within.

To hide this knowledge is spiteful and destructive, it suffocates and starves until it is of no use to those who steal it. Share and expand, giving freely and without expectation of reward, bring forth a beauty that is beyond description filling the giver with so much love, and the rewards that we receive will be decided by the way in which we give. Our acceptance of all that surrounds us and the use of the eternal and universal energy to fulfil not just our lives but that of others is now the responsibility of each and everyone of us who has the knowledge and strength of the Spirit within.

CHAPTER TWO

Give me the healing of the mind, give me the healing of the soul. The body can be healed in so many different ways by those who practice the various forms of restoration of the physical well-being of the human race. We complain with the sound of complex speech, but there are those life forms that do not have the luxury of human speech to enable them to communicate with those who would change their lives and environment. Take care my friends that we do not forget, when we ask for our channels to be used for healing, that there are many life forms that we have changed in order to provide the human race with its selfish desires. Take care we do not forget them: the animals, the birds, the reptiles, the plants, the trees, the land, and most of all the unseen damage we cause through greed, by raping mother earth of her riches in order to profit ourselves.

The mind, soul and spirit are all too often neglected when we seek healing; taken for granted sometimes, when, all too often we can overcome a great majority of our physical disabilities by remembering that a healthy mind can better channel the energies to the troubled parts of the body; a healthy spirit can more effectively channel thoughts through a healthy mind and a healthy soul can bring about so much beauty and light to cleanse the spirit within and so make us fit instruments to carry out the healing ministry of our Lord.

To use healing in order to help others is one of the great gifts made available to use by the Creator, allowing us to sometimes make changes in the lives of other people on this earth, thereby bringing about a greater understanding in those people of the importance of our thoughts and deeds and how they affect all life universal.

Now we are starting to understand the power of life energy we can start to use it in a more effective and positive way. For example, when we are linking in thought to send out our healing (be it animal, mineral, or vegetable, that we direct ourselves to), do not be tempted to fill that thought with negativity by feeling pity or sorrow.

Pity and sorrow are the mechanisms by which natural Law triggers our compassion, telling us to send out our thoughts, but all too often we send out pity and sorrow, when we should be sending out positivity, energy, joy and light so that when we make that link the recipient feels rejuvenated and not sad and sorry for themselves. This will do them no good, it is negative thinking, a destructive force that should not be present when we are attempting to bring about a healing condition with that with which we link. Sending the love and happiness that is so natural and wonderful brings with it fulfilment and healing.

CHAPTER THREE

There are few in this world who can reconcile themselves with the true facts. Sometimes we say we accept them, but in our hearts we hold a fear, because we do not understand them and our automatic reaction is to defend ourselves against the humiliation cast upon us by those who also delude themselves into believing that they understand. In order to promote themselves above others, they use falsehoods to trick us into believing that they have a greater knowledge and understanding.

This has the effect of making us believe we are subordinates and should do as they say. This is not necessarily so, we should question in our minds when others ask us to do their bidding: Are their intentions honourable? Are their intentions sincere? Do they fully understand the subject that they are dealing with, and the implication thereof, if they are acting in ignorance? Do these people who act in such a way, whether through ignorance, fear, or deceit, realise the damage that could be caused to those whom they are trying to influence, to the environment around them, to the universal energy that will be tainted by their actions, by the way in which they are defying natural Law, and how in return it will inevitably affect them and their progression?

Let us put forward to you this thought which, by its virtue, is a truth. We only wish to guide you and not to force you to do anything which you are not comfortable with, not to think in a way that is not truthful and honest.

A young girl is pregnant with no man to support her, her parents are not happy with this situation but will help her because they love her so much. She does not have many so-called good friends.

One day during a routine examination she is found to have some abnormality with the foetus, she is extremely frightened by the thought of giving birth to a handicapped child, her parents say that she should consider abortion.

Now we are faced with a decision which by nature would not normally have come about under natural Law. Men have for many hundreds of years interfered with things of which they have only limited or no understanding. Through what you call medical science, they have tried to cure ailments, treating only the condition and not looking for the cause, which in turn has led to greater complications as time has progressed, passing on their knowledge as they see fit to give; their opinion for as much as they could understand the things that they encountered; and so, the problems have become more and more complicated and as a consequence become more and more difficult to resolve.

The world is full of bacteria and disease which are becoming more complex and acquiring a greater resistance to the medicines that we develop. You see, if you devise an unnatural method of dealing with a problem, then nature can only evolve and mutate to survive the attack that mankind is waging on it. Natural Law defines that if something or someone acts in a way that is contrary to the normal order of things then an abnormal reaction will take place and the problem continues in a vicious circle of blind ignorance, which reaches a stage where not only is mankind plagued by illness and disease, but now through our foolishness we are affecting the unborn child in the womb and also before conception.

We are constantly acting in ways that are contrary to natural Law. Take the diseases we have at present that affect mankind in a drastic way: AIDS, Venereal disease, typhoid, hepatitis, herpes, and many, many more that we are not taking care in a responsible way to prevent their spread. This is contrary to natural Law. The way in which we destroy rainforests, scar the landscape with quarries leaving huge holes in the earth, mining for minerals and fuel without replacing what we take away, these are but a few examples of the mistreatment we carry out. Mother earth does not expect too much from you, but please consider the hand that feeds you, replace what you have taken, not with great riches as you see them, but with natural things, this is how we can, in return, feed our Mother

CHAPTER FOUR

Today we talk about the control of energy and how to use it to its full advantage for ourselves, but more importantly how to use it to help others.

During our everyday lives we use our bodily energy without thinking how we will convert the food that we eat and the air that we breathe into the movement of our limbs or the sound of our voice or the sight of our eyes. Do we even understand how the senses of our bodies convey the energy into conscious thought?

There are many great resources in this earthly existence of yours, yet mankind misuses it by trying too hard to convert such things as coal, oil, or gas into different forms of energy to provide for themselves the things that they think are necessary for them to live a comfortable life. We have seen, for example, a simple technique for providing us with a way of telling the time, without using valuable resources, over and over again. There are being suppressed and objected to such things as solar panel energy or wind generators, why…? This is not an unnatural form of energy, it is just that those who profit from the present forms we use are trying to safeguard their monetary security, how foolish!!

And so my friends to the subject of how we can harness and use nature's energy for our everyday lives and that of others also. Just imagine being able, when we feel exhausted, to tap into an energy source to enable us to continue with the task we have set ourselves and complete it successfully. First we must warn you that any abuse of this power for selfish or foolish means will only result in natural Law being unbalanced and so we will have to face and undoubtedly pay for the abuse or misuse.

Take firstly our diet and how we use food to maintain the bodily structure and functions. How much food do we need in order to do this? Do we overeat and store unnecessary amounts of fuel in our bodies? Do we eat the correct foods to provide us with the correct nutrients to use our body and mind effectively? This is also true of the soul or spirit: do we use it correctly to compliment our mind and body? Take as an example the most common form of use of the universal energy, healing! Shall we consider how this works? No, because we know that it works. Do not consider then how we can achieve a day filled with the energy we need to do the things we have set ourselves.

Sit now quietly and think of how we feel when we send healing thoughts to another person, do not analyze but just feel that same sensation, but instead of sending the thoughts out this time, send them in, into ourselves to the centre of our being and ask that it be issued to sustain us throughout our waking day so that all that we have to do may be done with ease and simplicity. Do not think of any particular task you have set yourself, just see yourself in a bright and happy mood full of energy not just for yourself, but when we think of someone or meet someone that we know, then we can think of some energy for them also.

We know that there are many minerals under our earth that provide energy, putting aside the ones we use for fuel, think of the crystals for example that we know have a vibration and energy patterns that are useful for different tasks, then realise now that all these vibrations are constantly around us.

When we need an energy boost to direct to someone or something other than ourselves then just create within your mind and around your body the feeling we use for sending out healing thoughts, this we can do while walking down a busy street, practice and learn how to harness and use these wonderful things around us, it is a natural process.

The Creation was intended to interact and survive by providing for one another, do so and the fruit of your labour will bring you rich reward in the life to come. Remember once you have developed your own technique you must use it to help others also, do not hide it or it will wither and die.

CHAPTER FIVE

How many times do we pray to our God and not realise how close He is to us? How many times do we ask for help and not realise that He is helping us? How many times do we ask for His forgiveness and yet we cannot forgive ourselves? How many times do we pray that He be near us, when He is never away from us? How many times do we ask for guidance and not see the pathway in front of us?

We have many names for our Creator, we call Him God, Jehovah, Allah or the Great Spirit, we refer to Him in the masculine tense but this also is unimportant. What we must remember is no matter what we call our Creator, or mentor, or spiritual leader, it is more important that we feel His love within us and around us, to realise we are His children and He cares for us and tries to lead us, tries to make us the best that we can be, but we miss the signs, we miss the steps along the way that he has prepared for us.

God is to us some unreachable magnificence who we call to in times of trouble, but we must not see Him as an existence outside ourselves, He is inside everyone of us, He is our friend and helper, not a stranger or a distant being who we do not know.

Do not look at God in fear, but fear God, for His might is immeasurable, because of who we are makes Him also aware of the power that we possess, so use your thoughts wisely, let God be your friend, feel His presence in and around you, let Him love you and love Him freely and without inhibition, without restriction, let Him touch your spirit deep within and feel the power of love, the excitement of being alive, the happiness and elation that He can bring you through yourselves. He is your friend and Father, talk to him and He will talk to you, let Him not be a stranger anymore and you will not be a stranger to yourselves.

Feel glad that you know God and pray with all your heart that others around you will realise that He is a part of them also. Go my friends and rejoice in the life that you have, for it is sacred and it is precious, care for it and help it grow in the same way as a young child, or a young animal, or a young plant. Nurture it and the fruits it bears will feed you now and evermore.

CHAPTER SIX

Let me take you to the spirit realms of light and colour; so intense and bright that it will at first hurt and strain your human eyes to gaze upon something magnificent and yet, to those who study and dwell within the enlightenment of our Creator, it is the most natural state of being, so simple to us for this is where we live.

Come with me now and I will fill your very being with so much joy, so much love and so much contentment that the search for the knowledge that you think is right and of benefit, will seem insignificant.

When we start our search from the physical earth plane, we seek that which we think we will be able to pass on to others of our world, in order that they may benefit from the knowledge that we have so graciously bestowed upon them. This is foolish and conceited of us to think that we have the right to advise others of that which we consider to be of virtue. Open your soul to the eternal truth that will be the guiding light of each individual to experience for themselves, not the ignorant interpretation of one who seeks to glorify themselves.

There are natural Laws laid down by our Creator that govern and interact with everything that we do as individuals whilst on this physical plane and, unless we start to realise that we must strive to help others to find the truth that they themselves must experience, then we shall be eternally responsible for any misguidance that we give in order to make ourselves seem greater in spirit beside them.

Tell others, without reward, how you have found the inner-self, the peace, the guidance, the love, the gifts that are given so freely.

Tell them how to learn within oneself of the spirit within, of the life within, of the knowledge within, the place where they will find their God. Do not seek of knowledge, but let the knowledge seek of you, to find that in searching so intensely we bypass all that life has to offer. Do not seek in narrow hallways the knowledge that you perceive to be that which will enlighten you, but seek to be a pupil of those who would choose to be your teacher. Trust them to guide you to a level of understanding that is beyond the conscious, logical, human mind, to a level where to learn will be your goal and all that is given to you will be understood; to give you the tools you need to furnish your existence on the physical plane; to furnish your progression through your spiritual journey; to bring about a mind that is clear and unselfish; to want for others what they should have, the existence that you have discovered by the acceptance of your life.

Let me tell you a tale of learning where a young student, in the realms of spirit, strove for knowledge, sought out the teachers and masters to enlighten him in all aspects of the universe and beyond, to fill his mind with the information and wisdom that they had.

He was unhappy; discontent that those he sought out could not help him learn fast enough, for he was young and enthusiastic, quick and impatient. Then one day he came upon an old white-haired man who sat staring at a goldfish in a bowl.

'Why do you stare old man?' asked the youngster.

'Because I am learning,' said the old man.

The young student could not understand this, but all the same was intrigued. 'What is it you seek?' he asked.

'Knowledge,' he replied.

'May I?' asked the young student as he indicated to sit with the old man.

After some time the young student became impatient, fidgeting and moving about.

'What is the knowledge you seek old man?' asked the young student.

'Study this goldfish for seven days and when I return tell me what you have learned.'

The old man returned after seven days and asked the young student what he had learned, to which he replied, 'Not enough! Come back and see me in seven weeks, by then I may have learned enough to tell you.'

The old man returned after seven weeks, but was sent away for seven years and when he returned the young student said, 'I have learned so much from this goldfish and yet I desire more, for every new day that dawns brings new life and knowledge so I shall continue to study until I am fulfilled.'

One day while the young student sat staring at the goldfish a voice behind him asked, 'Why do you stare old man?'

The young student looked surprised, but when he looked down he saw he had become an old man, he replied to the young student, 'Because I am learning.'

CHAPTER SEVEN

O Great Spirit, giver of all things, bring to us now your light, your love, and your truth that we may know of that which we are destined to receive, and that which we are destined to be.

Take me to the world of spirit, to the places where wisdom is taught, teach me how to receive your wisdom, teach me how to know You. Tell me of the things that you would have me learn in order that my life be true, show me how to bring truth to the minds and spirits of those who will seek out the givers of truth.

Come now to the world of spirit and I will show you things that are at present beyond your comprehension, beyond the belief of the waking mind, to a height that cannot be scaled by your world.

Gama says that the gifts are free for those who are free to take them, but for those who have no freedom they must pay the price of personal sacrifice to gain the freedom to enable them to be able to find the gifts.

Come to me and I will help you to find your own pathway to an open mind that will reveal so much to you that those around will find difficult to understand. This must be taught with discipline to others in order that their minds become focused on the responsibility that these gifts bring, to be flippant with this knowledge can only lead to personal torment, in the knowledge of these gifts one becomes more aware of the effects that they have when used correctly or incorrectly.

Be still my friends for in the silence there is an opening to the inner self, where one can find the doorway to the spirit within that is the centre of learning for the self.

We know when we are doing right and wrong, but we sometimes find it more convenient to take the easy option. So which is the right way to act? Well, listen to the spirit within, it will tell the conscious mind how to act and it will feel easy on your hearts when we experience this.

There are, and have been, many times in our lives when we have done things that we feel so good about, things that make us feel so uplifted that we know that we have achieved something. There are times when we feel so bad about things that we have said, done or thought.

Here is the key to the inner self, to be able to make decisions without having to ponder for many hours or days before resolving things, to be able to do and say and think with a clear mind, to be able to rely on the inner self to act in a natural way, to feel the freedom of the spirit to know what we have done, said, or thought has in some way brought someone else closer to their own truth, so that they may in some way find the peace inside that you feel when you make your decisions.

Words alone cannot explain the meaning of life and our purpose here, because we are all individual and have chosen different styles, only the self can determine the absolute truth. This is so because truth lies at the centre of love, whereby the access to this is by finding a way to give unconditionally with your heart, a task which may be beyond the material plane, because in this physical world there are so many restrictions that you submit to because you do not realise the full potential of the spirit within to achieve such greatness; you convince yourselves that it is unachievable.

Spirit does not place this out of reach. In fact, we are always trying to bring the two closer together by the guidance that is given in the form of clairvoyance that you practice in your gatherings. There are other forms such as writing and preaching, but you all to often fail to comprehend the root of the message contained within this, and are therefore mistrusting of the information that is available.

Why in this material world do you always criticize the words of others? This is not a good form of thought, it harms both sides because of the negativity it creates around you both, so that it shuts off the access to the absolute truth that you seek. It is there all around all the time waiting to be found, waiting to be nurtured by each and every one of you, find the self, find the peace that will guide you through the mist to bring you to that which you all have a right to.

God's love is free to all. He gives it unconditionally, and yet we are too blind to see it, to find it in the mists of the conscious mind that you fill with the clouds of material solutions to all that you have around, when truly the solution lies within the truth that you deny yourselves, through the fear that you hold in your hearts that the truth will harm you. Fear not, be brave and take the truth to those who refuse to listen and tell them they have a responsibility not only to themselves but to others, for they shun the truth because they fear the responsibility that it brings with it.

Do not be harmed by the harsh or stupid words of others. Take these words, for with them comes an energy that the other poor soul emits. Use the energy, not in its present form of negativity, but change it to love and give some back to the unfortunate abuser, so that they may benefit from being touched by something of beauty that you have created because you believe in your God.

CHAPTER EIGHT

Show me now your love, my friends. Show me that within you which is pure and priceless, do not pretend to love someone or something, love them unconditionally, love them from your heart that they will know and, if they cannot feel it, love them even more because they need to feel love around them.

Love will be your leader, love will be the sense of all things, in so much as when you are able to give love to your friends and family they will feel happy without a word passing between you.

Love your enemies that they may feel how good it is compared to hatred, let them feel the touch of your heart within theirs, that they will experience that which you experience, to make them more able to bring about the change that they seek within their hearts, to make their lives more fulfilled, to be able to love others instead of casting misery and hatred among those who they have tormented. Send out your love to those they have tormented so that they can find forgiveness of those who trespass against them, so that they do not wish, with anger and hatred, awful things to come about. This will only lead to more destruction, destruction of the soul and eventually of one against the other.

Create a greater love amongst yourselves by letting it flow all around you when you sit in your meditation, letting it emanate from every part of the spirit within to touch all those around you and share with the love that they are giving also, to make it grow as it bonds with one another, to make it stronger because it has no condition to it, it is free from restriction and is able to expand, to explode in a burst of happiness beyond understanding, so great that we feel alive within. Your bodies shiver with excitement when it is touched by this love and you feel so content that nothing can spoil the moment.

Harness this feeling within, it is a feeling of goodness and greatness, but not of importance and does not make you better than anyone else, you are just more able to feel and appreciate this love and are therefore better equipped to send it out to others who need it.

Bless you, my friends, that you enable others to benefit. There will be no reward or gain for this, it is not an exercise to bring about any return for the purpose of the self, but an exercise in giving, and giving alone, to learn to give and not receive. It is a lesson that brings with it humility and humbleness for who are you that you should receive a reward for giving something that does not even belong to you, but belongs to those who do not have it?

CHAPTER NINE

Guide me, my father, my Creator, maker of all things so that in my service I may serve You in honesty and truth, so that all people may know that it is only through your will we will come to know the beauty of our lives.

Help us in deed Dear Father that we should know only compassion for our fellow beings, only compassion for this our existence, a mere speck of Your Creation, that the love we do not yet know may draw ever near us, bringing us ever closer to Your heart, the centre of all living things and all things dead For in Your eyes, Dear Lord there is no death, merely the transition to that heavenly place to be nearer to You.

Open now our minds and clear away the mist that prevents us from seeing the guiding light that we all know is the path of right, to follow Your light Dear Father that we may see the truth that has no deception or hidden meaning, only pure love, created by You for us to see. Give us courage to commit ourselves to a way of life that will compliment that which we already have, building upon our existence so far during this earthly life that we have undertaken.

Reveal to us now Dear Father the key within us that we all possess to unlock us from our fears and ignorance, our defiance and stupidity, that we as lowly souls are creating, preventing ourselves from following in the footsteps of the great teachers that You have sent before us, to lead the way into a life of fulfilment of the spirit within.

Teach us now Dear Father that we have nothing to fear from You, that from You, and only You, comes the divine guidance that we all seek in the emptiness of our confusion; a divine guidance that cannot be found in books and words. These are there for a broader purpose, but first Dear Father we need to find You within our spirit so that we will all know when the time comes for us to return home to You; that we have prepared ourselves in a suitable manner, not by wealth or position, but by service and sacrifice to all of Your Creation to make a more peaceful and harmonious life for those who are left behind, and also for those who are yet to come this way; that the way may become clearer for them simply by the sacrifice that we have made, to ensure that their pathway is a little clearer than when we trod, so that their lives will benefit from Your Eternal Love.

CHAPTER TEN

A greater time now is upon us, as mankind comes to realise the importance of the cultivation of the self-awareness that we all possess. Once mankind realises the true potential that lays within, then he will seek to find ways to use this power. It is the responsibility of people such as yourselves to make available the knowledge to others and to help them know that there is only one true way to inner peace and enlightenment.

There is only one way to bring about self fulfillment and satisfaction, this is through the giving of the self freely to others in their time of need; to love unconditionally all those who are a conscious part of your life. When we feel the negative vibration of wrongful thoughts from others, then we have a duty not to shut out this energy but to take it in and use it to strengthen ourselves and to send it back as love, and only pure love, without any thought or interference in the way it is predestined to affect another. This is the way forward to make real the potential we, who are already enlightened, have within and around us.

Once we have achieved this, we can also teach others the way to make the spirit within strong, to make our love strong, to begin to know that with strong love comes stronger love, and so the energy of positivity will grow and grow far greater than ever we can imagine.

There is of course now to be told of the greatest sacrifice of all that we must make and that is, when we leave the earthly plane of this existence, then we must leave behind us all the love and strength that we have acquired during our earthly work and start afresh from the world of spirit – to strive to work through different channels that have different vibrations; to try to bring about the same result that we so easily found on the physical plane. This may seem strange to you at this moment, but you will find out when your time comes that to make oneself clearly understood to those who are called 'mediums' on the physical vibration is a much harder task than one first thinks, because of the lack of physical speech that we once had the luxury of to communicate with one another and to compare messages of a similar nature to those that other mediums have been given. But here in the world of spirit we are trying to teach on a one to one basis, and this can all too often be a one-way communication, whereby the medium does not always grasp the concept and therefore does not discuss the matter with their spirit teacher, but will try to fathom it out with someone else on the physical plane who is experiencing the same problem. So, my friends, learn as much as you can about the reality of thought vibration and thought communication, this will strengthen your love and make you more familiar and better equipped to fulfil your hopes and dreams.

CHAPTER ELEVEN

My friends, it is not our place to tell our fellow man what and what not to do, but to encourage him in his efforts if he is in pursuit of perfection and progression of himself in a manner of selflessness that, through his endeavours, others may benefit in the way of love and kindness. He should give of himself freely without precondition to the benefit of the world that he reaches.

Progression need not be of an holier than thou nature.

Perfection need not mean to become faultless.

To progress in one's life is to seek that within which can be cultured to enhance the entire being, to enrich and enfold the knowledge of everyday life that is his to behold. When each day arrives, the way that we live it is all part of our progression.

To perfect one's being is to be able to understand what is happening to you and to others. How you affect others and how they affect you. To be able to see why faults occur, why we lose our tempers, why others lose their tempers with us. To appreciate why one person loves another in whatever way, to see how the things we do harm others and to endeavour to stop and rectify (not always succeeding).

If in our hearts we are truly committed to trying and never ceasing to try, then we cannot fail, there is no failure, merely a lack of success, because we have the opportunity with life on earth to try, try again. Every day of our lives is an opportunity to enrich our lives, we are all individual and there is nothing in this world that can take away that which exists in our own minds.

Each one of us is a free Spirit with free will to do as we please, to save or waste our selves, but all the time our minds are our own. No one on earth knows what we think and no one on earth can make us tell them what we think, because no one can really know what we are thinking. So go now and work at your own being, your own self, make as great as possible your existence on this earth.

This book is the result of a lot of persuasion, even more encouragement, and even more down-right insistence on the part of those who know better. Trying to convince me that I, of all people, might have something to say that may be of some useful contribution to the lives of others, not realising, as I should, that there are those of a higher intelligence who will, come what may, deliver to the most unsuspecting of us a task to perform. This time it was my turn and I hope that I have delivered it in honesty and sincerity, that what has been said in these pages has not insulted or offended anyone, if so, then please disregard it.

Yours in Love and Light.

36884887R00041

Made in the USA
Lexington, KY
18 April 2019